Hour Of The Dog

Hour Of The Dog

Miggy Angel

salò press

This collection copyright © 2020 by Miggy Angel

All rights reserved. No part of this publication may be reproduced, stored in a retrieval system, rebound or transmitted in any form or by any means, electronic, mechanical, photocopying, recording or otherwise, without the prior written permission of the author and publisher. This book is sold subject to the condition that it shall not by way of trade or otherwise be lent, resold, hired out or otherwise circulated without the publisher's prior consent in any form of binding or cover other than that in which it is published.

The Portal and *Ultraviolet* were previously published in Silver Pinion (www.silverpinion.org)

ISBN number: 978-1-9165021-9-2

Printed and Bound by 4Edge

Cover art by The Miuus Studio
www.themiuusstudio.com

Typeset by Sophie Essex

Published by:
Salò Press
85 Gertrude Road
Norwich
UK

editorsalòpress@gmail.com
www.salòpress.com

For The Elephant

Rust alighted on my tongue with the taste of a disappearance.

- Antonio Gamoneda

Hour of the Dog *is the mongrel at his snarling, growling best; voodoo taboo spooking up city-skin. Angel's visions & incantations of past-futurism pin-prick the pages; death by a thousand Tory cuts. He's scoping out the witching-hour of gentrified times, spent (s)kin-grafts, azul-utterances, slivers in silver-blue. These bastard poems should be branded into the shit-shovels those hipster cafes serve up on as existence-hex. Angel's bruising class-war crepuscular-zone mirage(s) are to be treasured as much as to be chanted. Every day. See you on the barricades.*

- Paul Hawkins, author of *Place Waste Dissent*

The space between memory and lived experience. Between setting (as the hyper-truth of place in literature) and actual place (especially as a site of erasure caused by the ever-disgusting force of gentrification). Between pleats that are "red and exquisite as death." Between "your name" and "your name erased." Those betweens create Miggy Angel's poetics of luminescent thumping zones. Via the relentless consonance and assonance of these poems (sonic lesions, of a sort!), sound becomes a tunnel through which to witness the violence of displacement. Keep Dog Eye. Experience the porousness of lyric, the glow of bones, the gloomy region of dusk's apocalypse and its wary children.

Property is always theft, but more so in gentrification, which seeks, so stupidly, to squeeze all the place out of a place. Hour Of The Dog *is watching.*

- Olivia Cronk, author of *Womonster*

A howl for our times. Our end times. And what an archive of the end times this collection is. The whole sequence is drenched in blue, the blue of longing, the midnight-blue of bruises, of wounds, the blue of sorrowing for a world that has been lost and a world that never was. We're left clutching at the entrails of dog-boy and the violence of the gentrification of his South London. Miggy frequently juxtaposes brutality and beauty to stunning effect: 'organs/resemble almonds adorning/the abattoir floor'. These are poems of disappearance. Of boys going missing, lost to the tide. And yet here they usher forth again, captured in Miggy's verse; archived, remembered. This collection reads like the black room of photography, to see in negatives the South London only those who grew from within its cracks would know.

- Jack Young, co-founder of multilingual literary collective *Anemone* and co-host of the literary podcast *Tender Buttons*

Table of Contents

Blue	1
Keeping Dog-Eye	11
The Lucent	13
The Portal	15
The Apocalypse	16
Ultraviolet	17
The Lesion Contingencies	18
Afterburn, Afterbirth	19
The Oracle	20
The Red Window	21
The Bird	22
The Ineffable	23
The Putrefaction	24
The Inkling	25
The Prelude	26
Dog-Eye Boy	27
Stray-Dog	29
The Trespass	30
The War	31
The Procession	32
The Pharmacy	33
The Chrysalis	34
The Changeling	35
Sleep, Immutable	36
The Ministry	38
The Milk Tooth	40
Armageddon	41
The Tenure	42
The Grave	43
The Wagon	44
Rouge Reprisals	45
O, Omens	46
Stone Stone Of South London	47
St. George's Circus, Sapphire	48
The Curse	49
The Womb	50

BLUE

In South London we called keeping watch, or looking out, 'Keeping Dog-Eye'. The one who kept watch would 'Keep Dog-Eye'.

I was the one who kept watch. The Dog-Eye Boy.

In the Chinese Zodiac, The Hour Of The Dog refers to the hours between 7-9pm. Dusk hours.

Dusk, or twilight, is sometimes called The Blue Hour for the spectral-cobalt quality of light between day's end and night's beginning.

At the Hour Of The Dog, I would Keep Dog-Eye for the bruised hues of The Blue Hour.

Canine vision, ancient, South London witness. Traversing the phantasmal terrain of ultramarine terrafirma to testament. Luminescent zone between diurnal and nocturnal.

Gentrification was the hour of the dog, the night that would never begin or end, the new day that, for South London, would never come.

O blue light that glowed phosphorous ghosts in our mouths. O blue light requite us.

KEEPING DOG-EYE

The Lucent

Hour Of
    The Dog. Dust
of the dusk
    hour. Covert

light covers
    London asphalt
and stone in
    the lucent.

Illumination
    of vision. Bones
glow through
    lesions

alight in
    neon. Anatomy
no longer zonal
    or organ.

Territory
    of feral
geometries. Trace
    the hare

of prophecy
    across violet
air. Vapour
    trails. Spells,

revelation,
    elation revealed
in convergence
    of bluetones.

Wingspan expanse
    of the mauve
mongrel hour.
    From laceration,

lantern become.
    Hour Of
The Dog. Begat
    God.

The Portal

Day, and its falling through
    itself. Trailing the legion particles
of morning, uncountable

    tentacles of noontime. London,
transmutation in moon-blue.
    Stone transistor broadcasting

alchemical spells, and you
    its loyal receptacle. Curriculum
of metropolitan delirium

    in bruise-hue at hound hour.
Studious, observe in abeyance
    this detritus syllabus. Pupil

with pupils ablaze, kindling
    like tulips. Death and its
diaphanous trick. From the vault

    came a voice, no mouth. Spoken
lexicon of light. Sapphire
    hieroglyphs, phosphorous

hexagons crown conurbation
    in cyan. Eyes, opals.
Portals, open. Listen.

The Apocalypse

    The porous event of our lives
rusts in orphic light. At
    dusk the day approaches

its phosphorous appraisal.
    You ask, What purpose praise
without point of convergence?

    In the caucus of corpses
she never asked what ratio
    the half-light radiates. Peruse

the ineffectual element at
    the axis, pursue blossoms
furious devotion through

    the end-times. At moontide,
saint shed skin, boat made
    of snakes shall sink. Upon

haunches or knees, apostles
    of apocalyptic radiance, violently
emanate violet.

Ultraviolet

Sleep is a pristine state. Hypodermic lamb
    leaping the gate of the skin. Love
is a phantom limb, always
    itching. The tenements attuned

our antennae to the testimonies
    of the territory. Borough was a bow
for the arrow of childhood.
    No gauze for the lost cause

of your days. Saliva mirrors
    quicksilver. When you open the home
of torso, or so they say, organs
    resemble almonds adorning

the abattoir floor. Past ultraviolet
    walk far enough into darkness, until
your body is enveloped in night, and
    you will never be photographed again.

The Lesion Contingencies

Tangle of intangible
    tangents. Only
the mouth conversant
    with death

shall speak. Night
    odours the word's
augur. Alphabet
    of portents. Tense

as neither past, future
    or present, but
solitary presence
    and the perpetual

circle of self, as
    infinite connection
of hauntings. Throws
    her arms wide

around the million,
    bleeding lesion
contingencies. The final
    embrace. First

    poem.

Afterburn, Afterbirth

    Under the tutelage
of hemorrhage, taut
    body turned undertow.

Tuning-fork personage
    opines bone anthem
to an open promenade.

    Awed meadows, aqua
marine adoration. Sentient
    enters the Earth

as exhibit-A, exits
    as X-ray. Blood
beacons reaching arms

    to armageddon. The child
that wakes, allows
    another day.

The Oracle

Every word awaits its weather.
        Feather from wing, song
of falling. Weight of utterance
determined by absence. Occult
    of electrified oracular occurs

        without evidence. Did the altar
open? The fruit detach from
the mouth? Silhouette, would
    you recognise the oracle, from
        its epithet?

The Red Window

New room, ancient
    decor. Upon
breath, host
    dissolves. Ghost

appears. Apparently,
    an apparition.
Another apple, or
    abhorrence.

Orchard, or Orion
    of trees. Colony
where the body
    breeds scars

under sky, until
    no skin prevails.
No person remains
    in the abandoned

abode of the form.
    From a distance
discerned red stains
    on glass windows.

The Bird

I had a bird once.
    The story begins.
I was once a bird,
    in dreams. Asleep,

to migrate. At
    the edge of reason,
mist mutates presence,
    accumulates

mysticism. The race
    to escape
is a labyrinthian return
    to the garden.

I had a bird
    once. The story
ends. No one's hearse
    shall surprise

the cemeteries.
    I was once
a bird. I surprised
    the skies.

The Ineffable

        Strangest night. White
light like death. Bell-tower
        minus bell, sleepwalker
with a knife. Thought's

        odyssey to unlearn
itself. In the carnival,
        the carnal incarnate. Upon
the pound, the dog

        become kennel. Ineffable,
illegible decibel sounds
        upon the tonsil. Opaque
rain, organ reclaims

        inheritance of instinct. Fable
unable to traffic its
        fiction. Your name,
is your name erased.

The Putrefaction

Insects licking dictionary
    pages. Catatonic
categories. Thought eccentric

    this optic of chance
over metrics. Empiricists
    rusting in hubris

of measurements. Sonata
    of data. Circus
of circular rationale and

    its concentric logic.
Decades decanted to
    decadence, putrefaction's

cadence translates as
    opulence. In happenstance,
heaven apparent. Order

    become apparition under
haphazardness. Moonlight
    magi manoeuvres more

voltage from black sky
    vulgar with vultures. Sage
seance of silence for

    a violent violet age.

The Inkling

Intuition omitted initiates forgetting.
        Rest assured red cauterised rose
no other life but the one squandered.
        Phosphorus abyss. Bystanders bypass
wildgrass where carcasses grow. Was

        our garden. At the end, ground was transcendence
of ground. Caesar's grand seizure
        under azure awning of dawn. Transgression
gestated in gesture. While searching
        for monsters become monstrous.

The Prelude

The harbinger lingers
    arbitrarily. Rare bell
rings only once. Low
    below the window

was called. Arced as bows
    bodies coerced
by cursed penance lurch
    over menace of metropolis.

Void provoked evokes
    a nest. Unafraid, form
and worm, assumes
    proportions of the offered.

Skylight, naked, genius-stimulus,
    winged-thing. May mournings
murder martyrs
    pardon ogres.

DOG-EYE BOY

Stray-Dog

     Was the Dog-Eye
Boy, bred by redbrick
     and debuted by debris,

to sear further than
     ether, seer and teller
of the concrete streets.

     Dusk dropped its nets, my
descent into Southwark's
     gullet of lowlight, eye

and tooth a blueprint
     of prophecy for Lambeth
asphalt and alabaster.

     Cardinals enter migration
in my palms, sparrows, stowaways
     and fugitives speak

through the spokes of my will's
     wheel. Crouched
in the crack-house crawl

     space, dusk's skirmish
with dust, I was witness.
     Clairvoyant, euphoriant

in vision, exuberant
     in testament, intuiting
incandescence.

The Trespass

South London concrete is consecrated
    and colonisers are trespassing upon sacred,
working-class terrain. By Dog Hour

    I witnessed the might of violet light, to paint
the vile theft of our council estates, the
    accrued criminal acquirement of our soma

locales, in golden coronas, condemning
    urban colonialists in terminal crowns of claret.
Neon, Neocene London's guillotine.

The War

No words
    when all is
wound, when

    mound
of London
    moulded into

talisman
    of our exile.
In vision

    I exhale
my expulsion
    return to

bestowal
    amongst
bone-blest

    asphalt
our presence
    in Lambeth

Southwark
    is war
to the

    gentrifiers.

The Procession

Annulled in annihilation. Another
    animal from the ash. Flesh and fur
a mask no more. Mesh of red shards
    amassed anatomy's tapestries. Took

to toes and bomb-totalled towpaths
    of bludgeoned roses. Teeth and ether,
terror-ridden wild ones run feral
    over deformed terrafirma. Colossus,

pronounced *procession*. End-times
    encircling the circus' circumference.
Foresight foresaw a shorn clan, skinless
    kin. Pleats red and exquisite as death.

The Pharmacy

Animal reflexes
    annexed. The machine
mimicked movements
    until human
became plastic
    mime machination

imitation in motion.
    Through the glass
doors of the pharmacy
    of revery, entered
the archive of memory.
    Red river, grime

auditorium. Riven under
    London, child-moles
inherit their station.
    Earth's molestation
enfolds us. Narcosis
    narcissus.

The Chrysalis

The planet clenched
    its jaw fist heart.
Elaborate architecture

    of bereavement. A line
was drawn in the sound.
    Nobody heard a thing.

Upland, defeat tilted
    on broken feet upon
a teetering precipice.

    The holster, its steel seed,
holy and heartfelt.
    World a red realm

drawn by the hand
    of a volatile child. What
use this chrysalis, if

    we never leave it.

The Changeling

        Again, the agony.
A groan, become
anatomy, then
    geography. Pain

gains ground, and
you its withered
        waving flag. The wind
wins. In the

assassin's sight,
    himself. Angel
chained to a
changeling. Half-torn

        infant turns violet
by dusk's
apocalypse. No
    parent but this.

Sleep, Immutable

The annals
    in analogue.
Apologists,

    theologists, rogue
somnambulists
    roam electric

rooms of antiquity's
    realm. Amazed
and amiss. The

    mission to accelerate
light's fissure
    descent

through the guards and
    gardenia of
the gradient. Here,

    where we absorbed
the proverbs
    of metropolitan

reverberations. Basilica
    of skin and
silicone, ghoul

    of glimmering atom
extenuates the form,
    exoneration

of existence. Repose
    of torn
ozone rose. Table

    where the mute,
immaterial male,
    bowed head

to abdication
    of absentia. Sleep,
immutable. Blue. Feral,

    female.

The Ministry

Tell me
    I belonged
among the
    mongrels.

Cartographies
    of cartilage,
hypodermic
    hieroglyphics

written in
    aquamarine.
Superstition
    as reproduction

of unction.
    Light's lament
consecrates
    concrete.

No longer
    skin, but taut
microfilm pulled
    over sinew

and bone. Son
    a cinema,
cinnamon reel,
    home-movie

of mortification's
      intrusions. Mother
stirred the pot
      and the tide

beckoned blue's
      revival. Mourners,
venerable mirage.
      Fugitive light

ablaze
      the ministry
of absence.

The Milk Tooth

    Unable to recall our most valuable
recollections. Follow the red ribbon

    of memory, back into the wreckage.

Voluptuous voyage, return to the cage, its
    origin. Crosses of fire falling through

the black screen of night. Electric

    asterisk. Angel crawls through the blue
linen of the dusk-tombed childhood

    bed. Elope into the envelope of sleep.

Drowning kittens calling from the sandbed
    of your dreams. Cherubin enveloped

in rumination, rubies of nosebleed, opium

    spoons. Moon opening a mouth
with a tooth missing.

Armageddon

The fruit will not
    survive the orchard.
Graveyard where
    the final apple
fell. Night is
    cobalt. Regret

is white. Dot
    disappearing
in the palm
    of a red hand.
Advent of perspiration,
    waxen brow,

azure arrows for
    clouds. Crimson
resounds, madness
    ascends. Interpretation
flickers like a fire.
    In the theatre

of flame, some
    saw a stove, or
kiln. Some
    where to warm
the child's
    hands. Like

him, you see
    armageddon.

The Tenure

    Primordial signs corroborate
metaphysical presence.
    Subterranean veneer, obscured

by daylight, unveiled
    by dusk's resurrection. Light
delineates night in lines

    of primary blue. See no
shadow but souls strewn
    in neon directions. What dusk

devours of day will never be
    avenged. In nocturnal hue
skin become mauve regal

    architecture atoms angels
eternally recurring sentient
    of fearsome sensibilities.

Tonight, in violet light, surrender
    your tenure. Tend toward
tenderness.

The Grave

Of all the fates, light is most patient.
    Torch travails black halls of cold cosmos
for eternity. To paint your hour cerulean.
    We waited for weightlessness. Eight
listless millenia passed by just today.

    How the particulars burn. The vapours

curl like a prayer, ghazal of fractures,
    particles enact absence. Concrete
complicit in canned fluorescence. Azure
    fever, forever. Patient without cure. Violet's
gradient for a grave.

The Wagon

        Alone on the deserted road. Prone,
    blade of blue light, azure razor
over asphalt. Beneath a stalactite-white
    sky. Tribe shall never arrive.

        Bludgeoned body a port of
              unimportance, no ship of connections
    shall dock. Advancing music granted
only to the perpetual emigrant.

The calling of the fallen. Bloodied
    and bare palms divine the barren
        road. The ground is still warm. Without
            vision or icon, trail her invisible wagon.

Rouge Reprisals

Blunt enmity
    of anonymity.

Mitigates endless
    entities of envy.

Earnestness
    harnessed cemented

senses in concentric
    secretions. Secrecy

of decrepit sect
    detected. Inchoate

cohorts contort
    to subordination.

Strangeness echoes
    coherently among

the estranged throng
    flung far across

the chasm of the
    schism. Violet inlets

where pooled skulls
    unspool. Needful

kneeling in praise
    of rouge reprisals.

O, Omens

    Urged across shellacked surface. Cowed
cowards. Coerced by hunger towards
    convergence. On the verge, carnivores
bore down upon nexus unfurled. Fire

    scroll in a troll's palm. No icon, avatar
or psalm but legion scar upon darkside
    of deadstar. Us, useless. Faceless
as tails. Old odes corroded. Ground

    beneath feet secretes concrete promises
broken. No portals open to auteurs
    of light. Narcosis cloud alights chalice
smoke illuminates violaceous fluorescence.

    Eternal night of the carcass. Toothless
mouth, tomb tokens, dystopian omens
    opening and closing
like coffins.

Stolen Stone Of South London

By blue-moon down
      a hand scrapes
the landscape of its scars.
      Tongue traces asphalt
argot of betrayal. Stone
              of London, bone

of kin, emptied of its
      personage. Terrafirma
epidermis, concrete
      integument, shrouds
the heart of the South.
              Follow the cord

to the dischord. Heed
      the hordes' word. Shall
swallow the sword
      of insubordination
and breathe a blue fire
              to the colonisers.

St. George's Circus, Sapphire

By sapphire's shawl, I shall traverse
        a clockwise circumference, toward
and around St. George's Circus, encircle
        the spectral site by one hundred rotations, until

    time's scythe soothsays sages

        and saints, slays triumphal incumbents
of the gentrified Elephant, and
        to the remnants, the tenants and denizens
shall return home again.

The Curse

No bell tolls for what was stolen
    but the bones of the Cross Bones
Graveyard, resound like a drum
    in the tomb of my organism, and
the ground, upon which, dusk's

    violet light, bewitches the trespassers

in a curse for their incursions,
    shall witness the full circumference
of justice, returning to us, the children
    of Bedlam, our inheritance
bricks, and vengeance in incandescence.

The Womb

Hour Of The Dog.
    Porcelain dream
between sleep and
    death. Day, sleep

walking into night.
    Equinox creeps
through golden door.
    Eyes closed,

ghoul-hands held out
    in front. Day's thin-bone
fingers feeling for
    the afterlife. Indigo

glows, womb and
    warning. Wide whorl
aboard the under
    world. Obscene hue

alights hems of zone.
    Neighbourhood of
hooded children.
    Phantasms hood

winking death.
    Phosphorescence
resurrects.

Miggy Angel is the author of the poetry collections *Grime Kerbstone Psalms*, published by Celandor Books - *Extreme Violets*, published by Hi Vis Press - and *Boy, Bestiary*, published by Ice Floe Press. Miggy is the editor and founder of Burning House Press.